T0095879

FIVE TIPS TO SIMPLIFY DEFENSE

Holding the Weakest Hand at the Table

Audrey Grant

Five Tips to Simplify Defense
Holding the Weakest Hand at the Table

Baron Barclay
3600 Chamberlain Lane, Suite 206
Louisville, KY 40241
U.S. and Canada: 1-800-274-2221
Worldwide: 502-426-0140
Fax: 502-426-2044
www.baronbarclay.com

ISBN: 978-1-944201-32-6

Contact the author at:
betterbridge@betterbridge.com

Design and composition by David Lindop

Contents

Introduction

This Bridge Guide encourages players to see the potential of weak hands. When the defenders know the standard opening lead guidelines and how to use signals and the Defenders' Plan, they start to maximize the partnership's trick-taking potential on defense, even when holding the weakest hand at the table.

Part I – The Five Tips

Each tip is introduced with examples to illustrate the effectiveness of the tip.

Part II - A Collection of Instructional Deals

The basic and finer points of defense are introduced through sixteen carefully-constructed deals. The initial deals are straightforward yet complete with the basic ideas about good defense. They become more challenging. Deals #15 and #16, the Famous Deals, show how world-class players defend with weak hands.

The Bridge Quiz

On the odd-numbered pages, the Instructional Deals are shown in a Bridge Quiz format. The Suggested Bidding is included. The Bridge Quiz poses a challenge for the defenders. Turn the page to see the answer on the even-numbered pages.

The Glossary

Italicized words in the text are defined in the Glossary, with page references to where the terms first appear.

Bookmarks

Essential ideas are summarized on four bookmarks.

The Defenders' Plan bookmark can help defenders get into the habit of making a plan before playing to the first trick. This bookmark can be placed over the even-numbered pages, starting on page 22, opposite the Bridge Quiz on page 23.

The Five Tips to Simplify Defense bookmark can be placed over the odd-numbered pages when reading the answer to a Bridge Quiz as a reminder of the specific tip being applied.

There are two reference bookmarks: Opening Lead Guidelines and Signals.

Book Features

The Audrey Grant Bridge Guide series is published with the reader in mind. The two-color printing has hearts and diamonds in red, making the book easier to read. The binding method allows the front and back covers to be put together without harming the book. This makes it possible for the book to lay flat on the table so it stays open while reading.

We hope you enjoy your adventure with defense. Thank you for being part of Better Bridge.

Audrey Grant and the Better Bridge Team

PART I

THE FIVE TIPS

Know the Opening Lead Guidelines

The first critical point in the defense is the *opening lead*. The defender on lead sees only thirteen cards. However, information is available from the *auction* and opening lead guidelines. Even if the defender on opening lead has the weakest hand at the table, the card played to the first trick can impact the rest of the deal. Let's take a closer look.

Opening Lead Priorities

Lead Partner's Suit

If partner bids during the auction, the general guideline is to lead partner's suit. This is sound advice, whether defending against notrump or suit contracts. Partner likely has *length* and *strength* in the suit bid and one or more *entries* to help establish and take winners. Even with a singleton, leading partner's suit can be a good idea.

The next decision is to choose the card that best describes your holding to partner:

- With a singleton, there's no choice.
- With a doubleton, lead the top card.
- With three or more cards, lead low, from an *honor* or from low cards.

Consider this example:

DUMMY (NORTH)
♦ 10 8 3

WEST
♦ <u>K</u> 4

EAST
♦ A Q 9 7 5

DECLARER (SOUTH)
♦ J 6 2

West leads the ♦K, top of a doubleton, and then the ♦4. This *unblocks* the diamond suit, allowing the defenders to take the first five tricks.

With three or more cards in partner's suit, lead low from an honor:

DUMMY (NORTH)
♦ 8 3

WEST
♦ Q 7 2

EAST
♦ A 10 9 6 4

DECLARER (SOUTH)
♦ K J 5

If West were to lead the ♦Q, declarer would get two diamond tricks, one with the ♦K, and one with the ♦J. Leading low restricts declarer to one trick because East wins the ♦A and returns a diamond. West's ♦Q captures declarer's ♦J. Leading low also informs East that West has three or more cards in the suit.

With three low cards, West also leads low, the ♦2:

DUMMY (NORTH)
♦ 8 3

WEST
♦ 9 7 2

EAST
♦ A Q J 6 4

DECLARER (SOUTH)
♦ K 10 5

East is generally interested in how many cards West has in the suit. Leading low, the ♦2, tells East that West has three or more diamonds. This gives East reason to continue leading diamonds against a notrump contract. Even though South has the ♦K, East and West can establish four diamond tricks.

The Exception—Leading Partner's Suit After Raising

If West *supports* East's suit during the auction, East already knows West has three or more cards in the suit. On opening lead, West can further describe the quality of the support by leading the *top of nothing* with three low cards. In summary, if West supports East's suit:

- With no honor, lead the top card—top of nothing.
- With an honor, still lead low—low from an honor.

In this next example, West leads the top of a doubleton.

West	North	East	South
		1♠	1NT
Pass	3NT	Pass	Pass
Pass			

DEALER:	EAST
CONTRACT:	3NT
DECLARER:	SOUTH

North
♠ 10 9
♥ 10 9 5
♦ A J 10 8 5 4
♣ K 3

West
♠ 8 3
♥ K J 4 2
♦ 6 2
♣ 10 9 8 7 2

East
♠ A K 6 4 2
♥ Q 8 6 3
♦ 9 3
♣ A 5

South
♠ Q J 7 5
♥ A 7
♦ K Q 7
♣ Q J 6 4

West is on opening lead and chooses to lead the ♠8, top of the doubleton in partner's suit. East knows the ♠8 is either a singleton or a doubleton and West doesn't have a spade honor or West would have led it. West would lead the top of ♠K-8, ♠Q-8, or ♠K-Q-8.

After West leads the ♠8, consider the suit from East's point of view. East has five spades, dummy has two, and partner, West, has one or two spades. East knows South has at least four spades, including the ♠Q and ♠J. If East continues spades, the defenders get the ♠A and ♠K. Declarer, however, also gets two spade tricks, the ♠Q and ♠J. Declarer now makes the contract, taking the ♥A, six diamond tricks, and the ♠Q and ♠J.

East's best chance after winning the ♠K is to shift to a low heart, the ♥3, hoping West has three or more hearts, including the ♥K and ♥J. On the actual deal, the defenders can drive out the ♥A and promote two heart tricks. Along with the ♠A-K, and the ♣A, that defeats the contract before declarer can establish nine tricks.

West has the weakest hand at the table, yet West's ♠8 opening lead gives East the information to visualize how the defenders might take enough tricks to defeat 3NT.

Don't Lead the Opponents' Suit

It's a good idea not to lead a suit bid by the opponents.

Lead Your Longest Suit

The Priority is to Lead the Top of a Sequence

- *Solid Sequence*
  ♠<u>K</u>-Q-J-9-6-3, ♥<u>Q</u>-J-10-5-2, ♦<u>J</u>-10-9-4
- *Broken Sequence*
  ♠<u>K</u>-Q-10-6-4-3, ♥<u>Q</u>-J-9-7-2, ♦<u>J</u>-10-8-5
- *Interior Sequence*
  ♥K-<u>J</u>-10-6-3, ♦Q-<u>10</u>-9-5

There are exceptions. Against a suit contract, lead the top of two touching honors. For example, lead the ♦K from ♦<u>K</u>-Q-8-2. Against a notrump contract, lead low, the ♦2 from ♦K-Q-8-<u>2</u>.

Without a Sequence: Lead **Fourth Highest** from the Longest and Strongest Suit

The maxim to lead the *fourth highest* card from a long suit is used mostly against notrump contracts. While it may not seem to matter which low card is led, the fourth highest card has become standard because the *Rule of Eleven* can then be applied by partner. Subtracting the card led from eleven tells partner how many higher cards are in the other three hands.

Leading Short Suits

At times, against suit contracts, leading a short suit - a singleton or doubleton - may give the defenders a chance to *ruff* declarer's winners.

For quick reference, Opening Lead Guidelines are one of the bookmarks.

The first tip to simplify defense is:

Tip #1:   Consider the card to lead based on the auction and the opening lead guidelines.

Use Signals

The defenders exchange information about the unseen cards starting with the opening lead, which on most deals shows much more about a defender's holding than the single card placed on the table.

The defenders continue to exchange information to maximize their trick-taking potential in a deal by using three main *signals: attitude*, *count*, and *suit preference*.

Attitude

Using the attitude signal, the defenders show whether they like a suit through the size of the card they play:

- A high card, such as an eight or nine, is encouraging.
- A low card, such as a two or three, is discouraging.

After the opening lead is made, if the opening leader or dummy wins the trick, the priority for third hand is to show attitude toward the suit led. Consider this suit:

DUMMY (NORTH)
◆ 8 4

WEST
◆ **K** Q 10 6 3

EAST
◆ 9 5 2

DECLARER (SOUTH)
◆ A J 7

West leads the ◆K, top of a broken sequence, against a notrump contract. A low diamond is played from dummy and East plays the ◆2, letting West know East doesn't have an honor, the ◆A or the ◆J.

If declarer holds up and plays a low diamond on the first trick, West now knows, because of East's attitude signal, that continuing diamonds will give declarer two diamond tricks. West can shift to a different suit, waiting for East to gain the lead and play a diamond to trap declarer's ◆J.

Now consider this lead against a notrump contract:

DUMMY (NORTH)
♦ 4

WEST
♦ **K** Q J 6 3

EAST
♦ A 9 2

DECLARER (SOUTH)
♦ 10 8 7 5

The ♦K is led. Here, East plays the ♦9, an encouraging attitude signal, so West knows East has an honor, the ♦A or 10♦. West now leads a low diamond at trick two. East wins the A♦ and plays a third round, allowing the defenders to take the first five tricks.

It's a challenge for West to play a low diamond at trick two yet, if West continues with a high diamond, the suit becomes *blocked*. East can win the third trick with the ♦A but has no diamond left to lead. If East overtakes one of West's honors, the ♦10 in declarer's hand becomes a winner. It's a challenge for the defenders to take their *sure tricks* because they can't see each other's cards.

Count

We've seen one type of count signal used by the defender making the opening lead, and playing fourth highest. During the play of the deal, if an attitude signal is unnecessary, the next priority is to give a count signal. Here are the mechanics:

- A high card followed by a lower-ranking card shows an even number of cards.
- A low card followed by a higher-ranking card shows an odd number of cards.

Count signals can also be given by the defenders when declarer leads a suit. The defenders usually already know their attitude to a suit led by declarer.

The defenders often use a count signal when declarer is trying to establish a suit. Let's look at a deal where the count signal is used by the defenders when declarer needs to promote winners in the club suit, and then get to them.

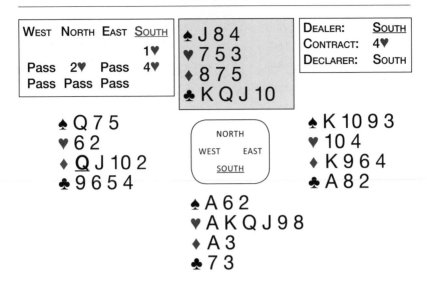

WEST	NORTH	EAST	SOUTH
			1♥
Pass	2♥	Pass	4♥
Pass	Pass	Pass	

DEALER: SOUTH
CONTRACT: 4♥
DECLARER: SOUTH

♠ J 8 4
♥ 7 5 3
♦ 8 7 5
♣ K Q J 10

♠ Q 7 5
♥ 6 2
♦ Q J 10 2
♣ 9 6 5 4

NORTH
WEST   EAST
SOUTH

♠ K 10 9 3
♥ 10 4
♦ K 9 6 4
♣ A 8 2

♠ A 6 2
♥ A K Q J 9 8
♦ A 3
♣ 7 3

West leads the ♦Q against 4♥, and declarer wins the ♦A. Declarer draws trumps in two rounds and then plays a club. Declarer needs to establish two club winners to make the contract.

West can see there is no need to give an attitude signal in clubs. West's attitude is clearly known. So the next priority is to give a count signal. With an even number of clubs, West plays the ♣9, starting a high-low signal.

A club is played from dummy and East has to consider the situation. West's high club shows an even number, either two or four. If West has only two clubs, it won't matter when East takes the ♣A because declarer would have four clubs, and entries wouldn't be a problem. However, if West has four clubs, declarer has only two. So East lets declarer win the first club trick. When declarer continues with another club, however, East wins the ♣A.

Now declarer is left with no link card to reach dummy's promoted club winners. The defenders get a club, a diamond, and two spade tricks.

When the opening lead is made and dummy comes down, the first signal given by a defender is typically attitude. If the defender's attitude is known, the next priority is to give a count signal. Here's an example.

WEST	NORTH	EAST	SOUTH
			1NT
Pass	3NT	Pass	Pass
Pass			

♠ Q J 5
♥ Q 5
♦ J 10 9 6 5
♣ A Q 6

DEALER:	SOUTH
CONTRACT:	3NT
DECLARER:	SOUTH

♠ K 10 7 4 3
♥ J 10 8
♦ A K
♣ J 9 4

NORTH
WEST   EAST
SOUTH

♠ 9 6 2
♥ 9 6 4 3 2
♦ 3
♣ 10 8 3 2

♠ A 8
♥ A K 7
♦ Q 8 7 4 2
♣ K 7 5

West leads the ♠4, *fourth highest* from the longest and strongest suit. The ♠J is played from dummy, East decides what signal to give. East's attitude is known since East can't beat dummy's honor. The most useful signal East can give now is count. East plays the ♠2, starting a low-high signal to show an odd number of spades.

Declarer has two spade tricks after the opening lead, one with the ♠J and one with the ♠A, three hearts, and three club winners. South's only hope to make the contract is to promote a diamond winner.

Declarer plays a diamond at trick two and West wins the ♦K. West knows East has either one or three spades. Since nothing can be done if East has only one spade, West has to hope East has three spades and South started with only two spades. West leads another low spade, the ♠3, and South's ♠A takes the trick. When West gains the lead with the ♦A, West takes three established spade tricks to defeat 3NT.

The defenders must be on the same wavelength to know which signal should be given in various situations. If attitude doesn't apply, count is usually the next priority.

When neither attitude nor count apply, a suit preference signal can be used.

Suit Preference

When neither an attitude nor count signal is needed, a suit preference signal can be given, following this guideline:

- A high card shows preference for the higher-ranking of the 'obvious' suits.
- A low card shows preference for the lower-ranking of the 'obvious' suits.

This is best seen through an example.

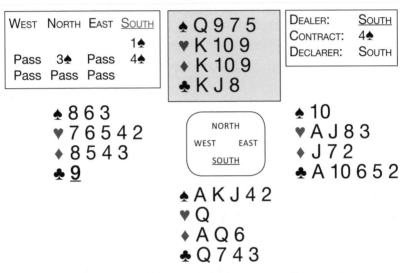

West	North	East	South
			1♠
Pass	3♠	Pass	4♠
Pass	Pass	Pass	

♠ Q 9 7 5
♥ K 10 9
♦ K 10 9
♣ K J 8

DEALER: SOUTH
CONTRACT: 4♠
DECLARER: SOUTH

♠ 8 6 3
♥ 7 6 5 4 2
♦ 8 5 4 3
♣ 9

NORTH
WEST   EAST
SOUTH

♠ 10
♥ A J 8 3
♦ J 7 2
♣ A 10 6 5 2

♠ A K J 4 2
♥ Q
♦ A Q 6
♣ Q 7 4 3

On this deal, West, with not a single high card, has two critical decisions to make during the defense: the choice of opening lead and which card to play to trick three.

West's best lead is the singleton ♣9, hoping to get one or more defensive ruffs. Now comes the challenge for the defenders. East wins the first trick with the ♣A and assumes West has no clubs left. After getting a ruff, West won't want to lead a trump, so West's choice will be between hearts and diamonds. East deliberately returns the ♣10 as a suit preference signal for hearts, the higher-ranking of the 'obvious' suits. The defenders take the ♣A, a club ruff, the ♥A, and another club ruff to defeat 4♠.

The defenders need to be familiar with attitude, count, and suit preference signals. They can also exchange information about their honor holdings.

Honor Signals

Defenders often exchange information by leading the top of an honor sequence. For example, the lead of the ♥Q tends to show the next lower-ranking honor, the ♥J, and deny the next higher-ranking honor, the ♥K.

This same pattern can be used when a defender plays an honor, not to win the trick, but to give a signal. Consider this situation:

DUMMY (NORTH)
♦ A 9 4

WEST
♦ K 6 5 3

EAST
♦ Q J 7

DECLARER (SOUTH)
♦ 10 8 2

If West leads the ♦3 and declarer plays the ♦A from dummy, East can signal with the ♦Q, showing the ♦J and denying the ♦K. This gives West a chance to know that West can get to East's hand later by playing a low diamond over to the ♦J.

On the other hand, when a defender is trying to win a trick, and has a choice of equal honors to play, the defender plays only as high as neccessary. In the above example, if West leads the ♦3 and declarer plays the ♦4 from dummy, East plays the ♦J, only as high as nccessary to win the trick.

Both defenders need to be on the same wavelength to take advantage of using signals. One defender gives the signal, and the other defender has to be looking for it.

The second tip to simplify defense is:

Tip #2: Send appropriate signals and watch partner's signals to visualize cards in the unseen hands.

Apply Defenders' Plan

The defenders need to be creative when using the *Defenders' Plan*. They are at a disadvantage compared to declarer. For example, on the opening lead, the defender can see only thirteen of the fifty-two cards.

However, the auction, the opening lead, and the sight of dummy can help the defenders visualize how they might get the tricks needed to defeat the contract.

The defenders have to know the general opening lead guidelines and signals. Then they can apply the ABC's of Defenders' Plan.

Assess the Situation

Imagine how many tricks you need to defeat the contract and how many you have. Typically, count winners on defense because there would be too many losers to count. Suppose you are on lead against 3NT with this hand:

♠ Q 10 8 5 2
♥ 7 3
♦ 8 4 2
♣ A K 6

With no information from the auction, you can see two sure club tricks and three more tricks are needed.

However, if you are leading against a 4♥ contract with no useful information from the auction, there are likely two club winners and you will need two more tricks.

Once dummy comes down, the defenders know much more about the layout of the cards. Both defenders can make an assessment of the source of potential tricks and adjust expectations as the play proceeds.

Taking Sure Tricks

Declarer knows when there are enough sure tricks to make the contract. The defenders, however, have a challenge, even when they have sure tricks. Consider this layout defending against a notrump contract:

DUMMY (NORTH)
♥ 9 6 4

WEST   EAST
♥ **K** Q J 7 3   ♥ A 2

DECLARER (SOUTH)
♥ 10 8 5

It would be easy to take five heart tricks if declarer held the East-West cards. Declarer would take the first trick with the ♥A, high card from the *short side*, and play the ♥2 to reach the rest of the winners in West's hand.

It's more challenging for the defenders. West would lead the ♥K, unsure whether the partnership needs to develop heart tricks through *promotion* or whether the defenders have five tricks to take when East holds the A♥.

To take the first five tricks, East has to unblock the heart suit by playing the ♥A on West's ♥K and then leading the ♥2. If South held four hearts including the ♥10, that would cost a trick, but the defenders do the best they can, faced with not being able to see each other's cards.

Browse Defenders' Checklist

The defenders imagine how to take tricks using the same checklist as declarer. Tricks can be developed through:

- Promotion
- Length
- *Finesse*
- Trumping the Opponents' Winners

It's not always clear for the defenders which technique is being used. They have to be flexible and able to change plans as the tricks are played and more information becomes available.

Consider the Order

The defenders need to plan the order in which to play their cards. Consider this deal:

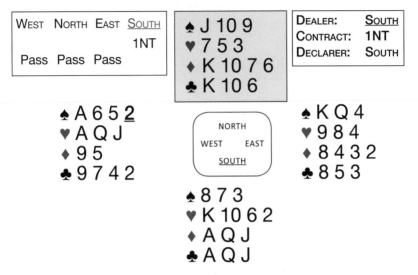

WEST	NORTH	EAST	SOUTH
			1NT
Pass	Pass	Pass	

♠ J 10 9
♥ 7 5 3
♦ K 10 7 6
♣ K 10 6

DEALER: SOUTH
CONTRACT: 1NT
DECLARER: SOUTH

♠ A 6 5 2
♥ A Q J
♦ 9 5
♣ 9 7 4 2

NORTH
WEST EAST
SOUTH

♠ K Q 4
♥ 9 8 4
♦ 8 4 3 2
♣ 8 5 3

♠ 8 7 3
♥ K 10 6 2
♦ A Q J
♣ A Q J

West leads the ♠2, fourth best from the longest and strongest suit. When fourth best is the ♠2 there are no lower-ranking cards, so East knows West has only a four-card suit. East wins the first trick with the ♠Q, playing only as high as necessary. With the ♠J-10-9 in dummy, declarer would presumably have won if holding the ♠A, so East can visualize West holds the ♠A.

East could automatically continue with the ♠K and another spade, and the defenders can take the first four tricks. Then, however, West would be on lead and have no good option for leading to trick five. Since neither East nor dummy has strength in hearts, East can anticipate West's problem. East can visualize West has some strength in hearts, and doesn't want to lead away from that strength.

At trick two, therefore, East should shift to the ♥9, top of nothing, hopefully leading through declarer's strength and up to the weakness in dummy. Assuming declarer plays low, West wins the ♥J and must consider the situation. West imagines East holds the K♠ because declarer didn't play it at trick one.

At trick three, West leads another low spade to East's ♠K. East continues by playing another heart. West can now win two more heart tricks and take two spade tricks to defeat the contract. Only by playing their cards in the right order can the defenders take all the tricks to which they are entitled.

That is a challenging hand but illustrates the defenders can make a flexible plan, and be willing to make changes if it seems the original plan isn't going to work.

On this deal, the defenders took four spade tricks, developing one trick through length in the West hand, and three heart tricks using the defensive finesse. The cards had to be played in exactly the right order.

The third tip to simplify defense is:

Tip #3:   Use the Defenders' Plan and visualize how to take sure tricks and get the extra tricks needed through promotion, length, the defensive finesse, and ruffs.

Adapt Defensive Maxims

Two popular maxims for defenders are *second hand low* and *third hand high*. Sometimes, however, they conflict with other maxims. You may need to consider additional maxims or adapt the ones you have. Let's take a look.

Keep an Entry with the Suit Being Established

East opens 1♥, South overcalls 1NT, and North-South get to 3NT. West leads the ♥9, top of a doubleton.

West	North	East	South
		1♥	1NT
Pass	3NT	Pass	Pass
Pass			

♠ 8 5
♥ 6 5 4 2
♦ A Q
♣ Q J 8 6 4

Dealer:	East
Contract:	3NT
Declarer:	South

♠ 9 7 6 3 2
♥ 9 3
♦ 10 4 3 2
♣ A 7

NORTH
WEST   EAST
SOUTH

♠ K Q 4
♥ Q J 10 8 7
♦ J 8 5
♣ K 2

♠ A J 10
♥ A K
♦ K 9 7 6
♣ 10 9 5 3

Declarer wins the first trick with the ♥A and plays the ♣3. The guideline for West is second hand low, and suggests West plays the ♣7. East wins the ♣K and drives out declarer's remaining heart stopper. However, East has no entry to regain the lead before declarer has nine tricks.

Instead, West must play second hand high and win the ♣A. West then leads another heart, driving out declarer's second heart stopper. Declarer can't take nine tricks without promoting the club winners. When declarer leads another club, it's East who now wins with the ♣K and takes the three established heart winners.

West followed a less well-known maxim: *keep an entry* with the long suit being established. In this case, the long suit is the hearts in East's hand. West plays the ♣A to protect East's ♣K entry until the heart suit is established.

Third Hand Only as High as Necessary

Although third hand high is a popular maxim, it must be extended with the proviso: third hand only as high as necessary. Consider this heart suit where West is on lead against a notrump contract:

DUMMY (NORTH)
♥ 9 2

WEST   EAST
♥ K 8 7 <u>5</u> 3   ♥ Q J 4

DECLARER (SOUTH)
♥ A 10 6

West leads the ♥5. If East plays the ♥Q to the first trick and declarer wins the ♥A, West may be reluctant to continue the suit after gaining the lead, worried declarer started with ♥A-J-6.

Instead, East plays the ♥J, only as high as necessary. If declarer wins the ♥A, West now knows East holds the ♥Q. Otherwise declarer would have won with the ♥Q and not the ♥A. So West has no problem continuing with a low heart on gaining the lead.

If East did play the ♥Q to the first trick, following this principle, West could be certain declarer holds the ♥J since East would have played the ♥J holding the ♥Q-J.

The fourth tip to simplify defense is:

Tip #4:   Use the defensive maxims: Second hand low; Third hand only as high as necessary; Keep an entry with the suit being established; Take the losses early; High card from the short side first. However, be aware of exceptions.

Prevent Declarer from Taking Tricks

Both declarer and defenders are trying to get tricks through promotion, length, the finesse, and ruffing the opponents' winners. A challenge for both declarer and defenders is to reach the tricks once they are established. For both partnerships, "entries are everything." Let's take a closer look, to see how the defenders can prevent the declarer from taking tricks.

The Hold-Up Play

Consider this layout. Declarer has the potential to promote four diamond tricks:

DUMMY (NORTH)
♦ K Q J 10 9

WEST   EAST
♦ 8 5 2   ♦ A 7 3

DECLARER (SOUTH)
♦ 6 4

If declarer has no entries to dummy in another suit, the defenders can prevent declarer from getting to the diamond winners once they are promoted. When declarer plays a diamond, East has to *hold up* playing the ♦A on the first trick.

When the declarer is playing a suit, there's no reason for the defenders to give an attitude signal since they both know this is declarer's suit. Instead, they can give a count signal. West plays the ♦2 to the first trick and East knows West started with an odd number of diamonds. Since it won't matter if West has a singleton, because that would mean declarer has four diamonds and could easily get to the dummy, East assumes West has three diamonds, leaving declarer with only two.

Declarer plays a second diamond and East wins the ♦A. Now declarer can't get to dummy since there is no link card left in declarer's hand.

Another time the defenders can hold up is when the declarer is trying a finesse. It's not always necessary to win the first trick, especially when declarer has no outside entries to the dummy. Consider this example where declarer is playing in a notrump contract:

DUMMY (NORTH)
♦ A Q J 8 5 4

WEST
♦ 7 2

EAST
♦ K 10 3

DECLARER (SOUTH)
♦ 9 6

Declarer leads a diamond toward dummy, planning to take the diamond finesse. West plays the ♦7 and declarer plays the ♦Q or ♦J from dummy. East could simply cover the honor with an honor and take the trick. A better idea, however, is for East to plan on holding up the ♦K on the first trick.

Declarer will now use an entry to get back to the South hand and repeat the finesse. This time, East takes the ♦K. Now declarer needs an outside entry to reach the established diamond winners in dummy. If declarer doesn't have an outside entry, the good diamond tricks are stranded in the dummy.

Keeping the Same Length as Dummy and Declarer

A useful guideline is to "try to keep the same length in a suit declarer may try to develop." Sometimes it is up to one partner to guard a suit. Sometimes it's up to the other partner to guard a suit.

Consider this next deal where East-West are defending against South's 6NT contract.

West	North	East	South
			1NT
Pass	6NT	Pass	Pass
Pass			

♠ A J 6
♥ K Q 5
♦ K Q 7 5
♣ Q J 9

DEALER: SOUTH
CONTRACT: 6NT
DECLARER: SOUTH

♠ 8 4 2
♥ J 10 9 4
♦ 10 8 3 2
♣ 7 3

NORTH
WEST   EAST
SOUTH

♠ 10 9 5 3
♥ A 8 7
♦ J 6
♣ 8 6 4 2

♠ K Q 7
♥ 6 3 2
♦ A 9 4
♣ A K 10 5

West leads the ♥J, top of the solid sequence, against 6NT. The ♥Q is played from dummy, and East wins the ♥A. East returns the ♥8, and dummy's ♥K wins the second trick. That establishes both of West's remaining hearts as winners.

Declarer next takes three spade tricks to which everyone follows suit. Then declarer takes four club winners. West has to find discards on the third and fourth round of clubs.

West can discard one heart winner on the third round of clubs, but has a challenging decision on the fourth round of clubs. Should West discard the remaining heart winner or a diamond?

West can't be sure whether it's necessary to keep the heart winner. East might have a heart winner. Looking at dummy's four diamonds, however, West can be sure it is necessary to hold on to all four diamonds. Declarer must have the ♦A and at least one more diamond, so West is the only defender who can possibly prevent declarer from taking four diamond tricks.

If West discards the last heart and holds on to all four diamonds, declarer can't take more than eleven tricks.

19

The fifth tip to simplify defense is:

Tip #5: Be aware of ways to prevent declarer from taking tricks, such as using the hold up play or keeping the same length in suits declarer is trying to establish.

PART II

A COLLECTION OF
INSTRUCTIONAL DEALS

The Bridge Quiz

The Bridge Quiz for each deal is on the odd-numbered page. To try the Bridge Quiz, first read:

- Suggested Bidding
- Opening Lead

Then consider the questions posed in the Bridge Quiz.

For the answers, turn the page to see:

- Suggested Defense
- Suggested Play
- Conclusion

For help answering the Bridge Quiz, put the Defenders' Plan bookmark, over the even-numbered page facing the quiz on the odd-numbered page.

After deciding how to defend the deal, turn the page over for the answer to the Bridge Quiz. Now put the Five Tips to Simplify Defense bookmark over the odd-numbered page that faces the answer as a reminder of the tip being applied.

In this Collection of Instructional Deals, declarer is always South, West makes the opening lead, and North is the dummy.

The dealer is shown in the upper left-hand corner and changes throughout the instructional deals.

Deal #1

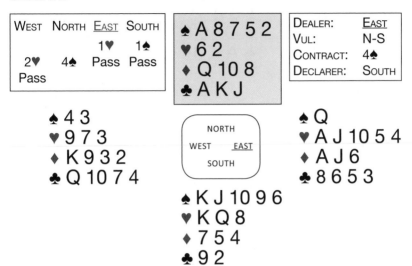

West	North	East	South
		1♥	1♠
2♥	4♠	Pass	Pass
Pass			

♠ A 8 7 5 2
♥ 6 2
♦ Q 10 8
♣ A K J

Dealer:	East
Vul:	N-S
Contract:	4♠
Declarer:	South

♠ 4 3
♥ 9 7 3
♦ K 9 3 2
♣ Q 10 7 4

NORTH
WEST   EAST
SOUTH

♠ Q
♥ A J 10 5 4
♦ A J 6
♣ 8 6 5 3

♠ K J 10 9 6
♥ K Q 8
♦ 7 5 4
♣ 9 2

Suggested Bidding

East opens 1♥ with 12 high-card points plus 1 length point for the five-card heart suit. South overcalls 1♠ with 9 high-card points and 1 length point for the five-card spade suit.

West advances to 2♥ with heart support and 5 high-card points plus 1 dummy point for the doubleton spade. North *raises* to 4♠ with five-card support, 14 high-card points, and 1 dummy point for the doubleton heart.

Opening Lead

West is on lead against South's 4♠ contract.

Bridge Quiz:

What impact will the choice of opening lead have on the trick-taking potential for the defense?

How can East take advantage of West's opening lead to determine the best chance to defeat the contract?

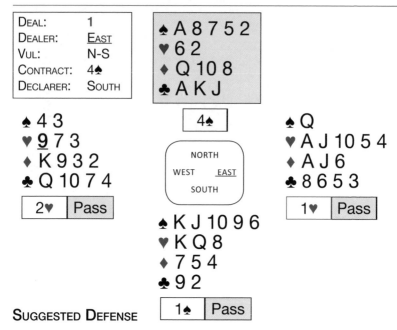

DEAL:	1
DEALER:	EAST
VUL:	N-S
CONTRACT:	4♠
DECLARER:	SOUTH

♠ A 8 7 5 2
♥ 6 2
♦ Q 10 8
♣ A K J

4♠

NORTH
WEST   EAST
SOUTH

♠ 4 3
♥ **9** 7 3
♦ K 9 3 2
♣ Q 10 7 4

| 2♥ | Pass |

♠ Q
♥ A J 10 5 4
♦ A J 6
♣ 8 6 5 3

| 1♥ | Pass |

♠ K J 10 9 6
♥ K Q 8
♦ 7 5 4
♣ 9 2

| 1♠ | Pass |

SUGGESTED DEFENSE

West leads partner's suit. Having shown support and holding three low cards, West leads the ♥9, top of nothing.

East wins the first trick with the ♥A. West's ♥9 lead makes it clear to East the defenders have no more tricks coming from hearts because South has the ♥K-Q. It's also unlikely the defense will get any spade or club tricks.

East's best chance to defeat 4♠ is to win the ♥A and shift to the ♦6 at trick two, hoping West holds the ♦K and South has at least three diamonds. This allows the defenders to take three diamond tricks to go with the ♥A.

SUGGESTED PLAY

If East doesn't shift to a low diamond at trick two, declarer can make 4♠ by discarding one of dummy's diamonds on a promoted heart winner, losing only two diamonds and the ♥A.

CONCLUSION

West's choice of opening lead is critical to the defense. The ♥9, top of nothing from three low cards, lets East know South holds the ♥K-Q. East can then visualize the winning defense and trap the ♦Q in dummy.

DEAL #2

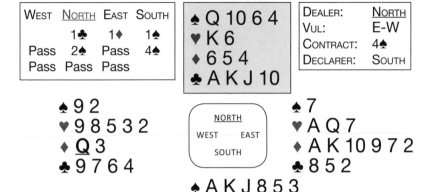

West	North	East	South
	1♣	1♦	1♠
Pass	2♠	Pass	4♠
Pass	Pass	Pass	

♠ Q 10 6 4
♥ K 6
♦ 6 5 4
♣ A K J 10

DEALER:	NORTH
VUL:	E-W
CONTRACT:	4♠
DECLARER:	SOUTH

♠ 9 2
♥ 9 8 5 3 2
♦ Q 3
♣ 9 7 6 4

NORTH
WEST   EAST
SOUTH

♠ 7
♥ A Q 7
♦ A K 10 9 7 2
♣ 8 5 2

♠ A K J 8 5 3
♥ J 10 4
♦ J 8
♣ Q 3

SUGGESTED BIDDING

North opens 1♣ with 13 high-card points and no five-card major. East overcalls 1♦, and South responds 1♠. West passes, and North raises to 2♠.

East passes. South, with 12 high-card points plus 2 length points for the six-card suit, has enough to go right to 4♠ once the spade fit has been found.

OPENING LEAD

West leads the ♦Q against 4♠, top of the doubleton in partner's suit.

BRIDGE QUIZ:

How does East plan to defeat the contract?

How can East communicate the plan to West?

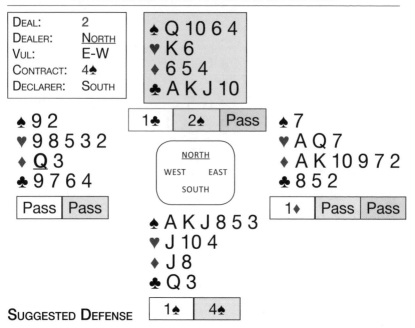

DEAL:	2
DEALER:	NORTH
VUL:	E-W
CONTRACT:	4♠
DECLARER:	SOUTH

♠ Q 10 6 4
♥ K 6
♦ 6 5 4
♣ A K J 10

♠ 9 2
♥ 9 8 5 3 2
♦ Q 3
♣ 9 7 6 4

1♣	2♠	Pass

NORTH
WEST   EAST
SOUTH

♠ 7
♥ A Q 7
♦ A K 10 9 7 2
♣ 8 5 2

Pass	Pass

1♦	Pass	Pass

♠ A K J 8 5 3
♥ J 10 4
♦ J 8
♣ Q 3

SUGGESTED DEFENSE

1♠	4♠

East likes diamonds but needs West to lead a heart at trick two to trap dummy's ♥K before declarer can discard heart losers on dummy's clubs. So, on the first trick, East should give a discouraging attitude signal by playing the ♦2.

When the ♦Q wins, it's tempting for West to continue with another diamond. West, however, must pay attention to East's discouraging ♦2 signal. East is unlikely to want West to lead a club, so East presumably wants West to lead a heart. West shifts to the ♥9, top of nothing. The defense gets two hearts and two diamonds to defeat 4♠.

SUGGESTED PLAY

If the defense starts with three rounds of diamonds, declarer can ruff the third diamond high, draw trumps and discard two hearts on dummy's extra club winners. Declarer gets ten tricks: six spades and four clubs.

CONCLUSION

The defenders need to use signals to take a defensive heart finesse. To defeat the contract, East must give a discouraging diamond signal and West must be watching.

Deal #3

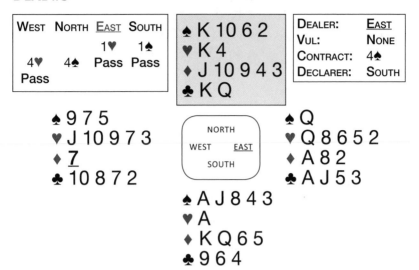

West	North	East	South
		1♥	1♠
4♥	4♠	Pass	Pass
Pass			

♠ K 10 6 2
♥ K 4
♦ J 10 9 4 3
♣ K Q

Dealer:	East
Vul:	None
Contract:	4♠
Declarer:	South

♠ 9 7 5
♥ J 10 9 7 3
♦ 7
♣ 10 8 7 2

NORTH
WEST   EAST
SOUTH

♠ Q
♥ Q 8 6 5 2
♦ A 8 2
♣ A J 5 3

♠ A J 8 4 3
♥ A
♦ K Q 6 5
♣ 9 6 4

Suggested Bidding

East opens 1♥ with 13 high-card points plus 1 length point for the five-card heart suit. South overcalls 1♠.

West has the weakest hand at the table but can make a preemptive jump to 4♥. The partnership has at least a ten-card heart fit and West has a potentially useful singleton diamond.

North has too much to pass and, with four-card spade support, chooses to bid 4♠ in case 4♥ is making. The 4♠ bid ends the auction.

Opening Lead

West knows the partnership has at least ten combined hearts, so the defense won't be able to take more than one heart trick. West applies the Defenders' Plan and leads the ♦7 against 4♠, hoping to get one or more ruffs.

Bridge Quiz:

What contribution can East make at trick two so the defenders can maximize their trick-taking potential?

What does West play to trick three and why?

Deal:	3
Dealer:	East
Vul:	None
Contract:	4♠
Declarer:	South

♠ K 10 6 2
♥ K 4
♦ J 10 9 4 3
♣ K Q

♠ 9 7 5
♥ J 10 9 7 3
♦ 7
♣ 10 8 7 2

4♠

NORTH

WEST   EAST

SOUTH

4♥	Pass

♠ Q
♥ Q 8 6 5 2
♦ A 8 2
♣ A J 5 3

1♥	Pass

♠ A J 8 4 3
♥ A
♦ K Q 6 5
♣ 9 6 4

1♠	Pass

Suggested Defense

It is expected that West would lead hearts, the suit bid and raised by the partnership. East suspects the ♦7 lead is because West has a singleton. East wins the ♦A and leads back a diamond for West to ruff.

Since East opened 1♥, West would usually try to get back to East's hand by leading a heart. East knows that won't work on this deal. To tell West to lead a club rather than a heart, East returns the ♦2 for partner to ruff. This is a suit preference signal for the lower-ranking suit, clubs. At trick three, West leads a club to East's ♣A and gets a second diamond ruff.

Suggested Play

If West leads a heart after getting the first diamond ruff, declarer wins, draws trumps, and loses only three tricks.

Conclusion

Both defenders apply Defenders' Plan to imagine their trick-taking potential. They use a suit preference signal to figure out how to get two diamond ruffs.

DEAL #4

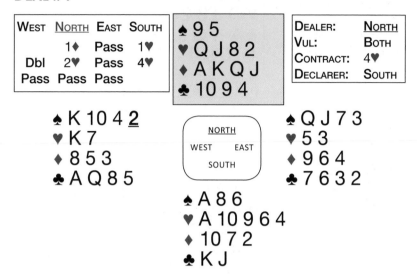

WEST	NORTH	EAST	SOUTH
	1♦	Pass	1♥
Dbl	2♥	Pass	4♥
Pass	Pass	Pass	

♠ 9 5
♥ Q J 8 2
♦ A K Q J
♣ 10 9 4

DEALER:	NORTH
VUL:	BOTH
CONTRACT:	4♥
DECLARER:	SOUTH

♠ K 10 4 2
♥ K 7
♦ 8 5 3
♣ A Q 8 5

NORTH
WEST   EAST
SOUTH

♠ Q J 7 3
♥ 5 3
♦ 9 6 4
♣ 7 6 3 2

♠ A 8 6
♥ A 10 9 6 4
♦ 10 7 2
♣ K J

SUGGESTED BIDDING

North opens 1♦ with 13 high-card points, East passes, and South responds 1♥ with 12 high-card points plus 1 length point for the five-card heart suit.

West has support for both unbid suits and 12 high-card points plus 1 dummy point for the doubleton heart. That's enough to make a takeout double.

North, with four-card heart support and a minimum opening, raises to 2♥. East doesn't have enough to compete and passes. With 13 points and having found a heart fit, South takes the partnership to game in hearts.

OPENING LEAD

West doesn't want to lead either of the opponents' suits and doesn't want to lead away from the ♣A. West chooses to lead the ♠2.

BRIDGE QUIZ:

How will the play go to the first trick?

How will that help the defense take all the tricks to which it is entitled?

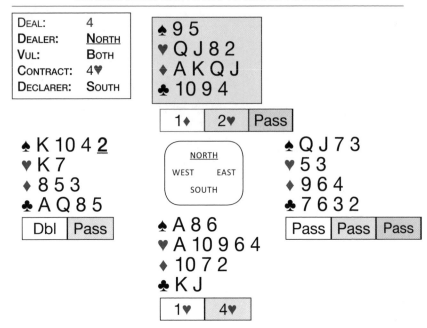

DEAL:	4
DEALER:	NORTH
VUL:	BOTH
CONTRACT:	4♥
DECLARER:	SOUTH

♠ 9 5
♥ Q J 8 2
♦ A K Q J
♣ 10 9 4

1♦	2♥	Pass

♠ K 10 4 2
♥ K 7
♦ 8 5 3
♣ A Q 8 5

Dbl	Pass

NORTH
WEST   EAST
SOUTH

♠ Q J 7 3
♥ 5 3
♦ 9 6 4
♣ 7 6 3 2

Pass	Pass	Pass

♠ A 8 6
♥ A 10 9 6 4
♦ 10 7 2
♣ K J

1♥	4♥

SUGGESTED DEFENSE

When the ♠2 is led and a low spade is played from dummy, East plays third hand high, trying to win the trick for the defense. With touching honors, however, East plays the ♠J, only as high as necessary. When declarer wins the ♠A, West knows East must hold the ♠Q.

Declarer crosses to dummy with a diamond to try the heart finesse, which loses to West's ♥K. Now West plays the ♠4 to East's promoted ♠Q. East can lead a club, following the maxim to lead through strength and up to weakness in the dummy. This traps declarer's ♣K and allows the defense to get two club tricks, in addition to the ♥K and ♠Q, to defeat the contract.

SUGGESTED PLAY

After winning the ♥K, if West takes the ♠K, declarer, on regaining the lead, can finish drawing trumps and discard a club loser on dummy's extra diamond winner.

CONCLUSION

Playing third hand only as high as necessary helps the defenders set up a defensive club finesse.

DEAL #5

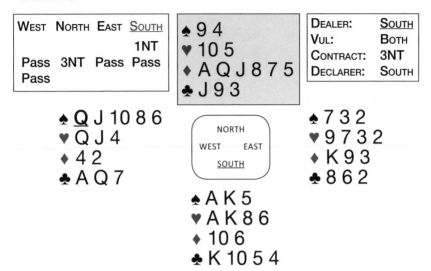

West	North	East	South
			1NT
Pass	3NT	Pass	Pass
Pass			

♠ 9 4
♥ 10 5
♦ A Q J 8 7 5
♣ J 9 3

Dealer:	South
Vul:	Both
Contract:	3NT
Declarer:	South

♠ Q J 10 8 6
♥ Q J 4
♦ 4 2
♣ A Q 7

NORTH
WEST   EAST
SOUTH

♠ 7 3 2
♥ 9 7 3 2
♦ K 9 3
♣ 8 6 2

♠ A K 5
♥ A K 8 6
♦ 10 6
♣ K 10 5 4

SUGGESTED BIDDING

South opens 1NT with a *balanced hand* and 17 high-card points. West passes. West shouldn't come into the auction with a balanced hand, especially when vulnerable. North, with 8 high-card points plus 2 length points for the six-card diamond suit, has enough to raise to 3NT.

OPENING LEAD

West leads the ♠Q against 3NT. This is the top of touching cards from a solid sequence. With nothing in spades, East plays the ♠2 to the first trick, as a discouraging signal.

BRIDGE QUIZ:

What can the defenders do to prevent declarer from taking nine tricks?

DEAL:	5
DEALER:	SOUTH
VUL:	BOTH
CONTRACT:	3NT
DECLARER:	SOUTH

♠ 9 4
♥ 10 5
♦ A Q J 8 7 5
♣ J 9 3

3NT

NORTH
WEST   EAST
SOUTH

♠ Q J 10 8 6
♥ Q J 4
♦ 4 2
♣ A Q 7

Pass | Pass

♠ 7 3 2
♥ 9 7 3 2
♦ K 9 3
♣ 8 6 2

Pass

♠ A K 5
♥ A K 8 6
♦ 10 6
♣ K 10 5 4

1NT | Pass

SUGGESTED DEFENSE

Declarer needs five diamond tricks to make the contract. After winning a spade, declarer leads the ♦10 and takes a finesse, hoping West holds the ♦K.

Although East is eager to win a trick with the ♦K and return a spade to establish West's spades, East can see that winning the first diamond will leave declarer with a link card to get to the established diamond tricks in dummy.

Instead, East should hold up winning the ♦K on the first trick. When West follows to a second round of diamonds, East knows that declarer started with only a doubleton diamond and can't reach dummy's diamond winners.

SUGGESTED PLAY

If East wins the first diamond, declarer has nine winners. If East holds up the ♦K and declarer repeats the finesse, declarer will get only one diamond winner!

CONCLUSION

In addition to trying to establish tricks for the defense, the defenders must try to prevent declarer from taking tricks. The hold up play can often be an effective tool.

DEAL #6

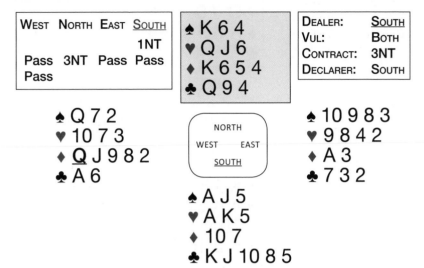

WEST	NORTH	EAST	SOUTH
			1NT
Pass	3NT	Pass	Pass
Pass			

♠ K 6 4
♥ Q J 6
♦ K 6 5 4
♣ Q 9 4

DEALER:	SOUTH
VUL:	BOTH
CONTRACT:	3NT
DECLARER:	SOUTH

♠ Q 7 2
♥ 10 7 3
♦ Q J 9 8 2
♣ A 6

NORTH
WEST   EAST
SOUTH

♠ 10 9 8 3
♥ 9 8 4 2
♦ A 3
♣ 7 3 2

♠ A J 5
♥ A K 5
♦ 10 7
♣ K J 10 8 5

SUGGESTED BIDDING

South opens 1NT with a balanced hand and 16 high-card points plus 1 length point for the five-card club suit. West doesn't have the strength or distribution to come into the auction. North raises to 3NT with 11 high-card points.

OPENING LEAD

West leads the ♦Q against 3NT, top of a broken sequence.

BRIDGE QUIZ:

What technique can the defenders use to defeat 3NT?

DEAL:	6
DEALER:	SOUTH
VUL:	BOTH
CONTRACT:	3NT
DECLARER:	SOUTH

♠ K 6 4
♥ Q J 6
♦ K 6 5 4
♣ Q 9 4

3NT

NORTH

WEST   EAST

SOUTH

♠ Q 7 2
♥ 10 7 3
♦ Q J 9 8 2
♣ A 6

Pass | Pass

♠ 10 9 8 3
♥ 9 8 4 2
♦ A 3
♣ 7 3 2

Pass

♠ A J 5
♥ A K 5
♦ 10 7
♣ K J 10 8 5

1NT | Pass

SUGGESTED DEFENSE

Although West's opening lead temporarily traps dummy's ♦K, if declarer plays low from dummy, East must be careful not to block the suit. From the ♦Q lead, East can visualize West is leading from a suit headed by the ♦Q-J-10 or ♦Q-J-9, so the defense can promote winners by simply driving out dummy's ♦K. East should overtake West's ♦Q with the ♦A and return the ♦3. This allows West to drive out dummy's ♦K and promote enough winners to defeat the contract while still holding the ♣A.

SUGGESTED PLAY

Declarer has two sure spades and three hearts. Four more tricks are needed and can be promoted in clubs. The only danger is the diamond suit. Declarer should play low from dummy when the ♦Q is led and also if the ♦J is continued. If East wins the second trick with the ♦A, the contract is safe.

CONCLUSION

East's only high card is the ♦A but East shouldn't let it get in the way of establishing West's suit. If West had led a low diamond, East would have no difficulty winning the ♦A and returning the ♦3.

DEAL #7

West	North	East	South
	1♣	Pass	1♥
Pass	2♥	Pass	4♥
Pass	Pass	Pass	

♠ K 7 4
♥ A 8 6 2
♦ Q J 5
♣ A 9 5

DEALER:	NORTH
VUL:	BOTH
CONTRACT:	4♥
DECLARER:	SOUTH

♠ J 10 9 3
♥ -
♦ A K 6 4 3
♣ 8 6 4 3

```
        NORTH
   WEST      EAST
        SOUTH
```

♠ 8 6 5 2
♥ Q J 10 9
♦ 10 8 2
♣ 10 2

♠ A Q
♥ K 7 5 4 3
♦ 9 7
♣ K Q J 7

SUGGESTED BIDDING

North opens 1♣ with 14 high-card points and no five-card major. South, with 15 high-card points plus 1 length point for the five-card heart suit, responds 1♥.

West might enter the auction with a takeout double but decides to pass with only 8 high-card points, vulnerable. North raises to 2♥, and South has more than enough to continue to 4♥.

OPENING LEAD

West leads the ♦A, top of touching high cards, against 4♥.

BRIDGE QUIZ:

When dummy comes down, what is East's plan to defeat the contract?

How does East communicate this to West?

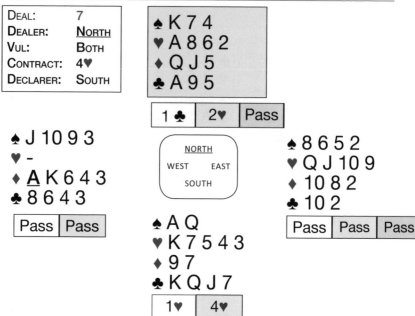

DEAL:	7
DEALER:	NORTH
VUL:	BOTH
CONTRACT:	4♥
DECLARER:	SOUTH

♠ K 7 4
♥ A 8 6 2
♦ Q J 5
♣ A 9 5

1♣	2♥	Pass

NORTH
WEST   EAST
SOUTH

♠ J 10 9 3
♥ -
♦ A K 6 4 3
♣ 8 6 4 3

Pass	Pass

♠ 8 6 5 2
♥ Q J 10 9
♦ 10 8 2
♣ 10 2

Pass	Pass	Pass

♠ A Q
♥ K 7 5 4 3
♦ 9 7
♣ K Q J 7

1♥	4♥

SUGGESTED DEFENSE

When West leads the ♦A and dummy comes down, East makes a plan. East has two sure heart tricks and West's ♦A is a third trick. West presumably has the ♦K as well and, if West takes it, that will be four tricks for the defense.

If East makes a discouraging attitude signal by playing the ♦2, West is likely to shift to another suit, hoping to establish tricks elsewhere for the defense. To make sure West takes the ♦K, East makes an encouraging signal by playing the ♦10 at trick one. After West takes the ♦K, East will eventually get two trump tricks.

SUGGESTED PLAY

If West shifts to a spade or a club at trick two, declarer can unblock the ♠A-Q and then discard the diamond loser on dummy's ♠K.

CONCLUSION

When dummy comes down, both defenders need to use Defenders' Plan. If a defender can see the best way to defeat the contract, that defender must try to communicate the plan to partner using the available signals.

DEAL #8

WEST	NORTH	EAST	SOUTH
	1♣	Pass	1♠
Dbl	2♠	Pass	4♠
Pass	Pass	Pass	

♠ A 10 6 3
♥ 8 5 3
♦ 10 8
♣ A K Q 10

DEALER:	NORTH
VUL:	NONE
CONTRACT:	4♠
DECLARER:	SOUTH

♠ 4 2
♥ A K 7 2
♦ A Q 9 4
♣ 8 7 3

NORTH
WEST   EAST
SOUTH

♠ 9
♥ Q J 9 6
♦ 7 5 3 2
♣ 9 5 4 2

♠ K Q J 8 7 5
♥ 10 4
♦ K J 6
♣ J 6

SUGGESTED BIDDING

North opens 1♣ with 13 high-card points and no five-card major. East passes, and South responds 1♠. West makes a takeout double with an opening bid and support for both unbid suits.

North, with four-card support for responder's spades, raises to 2♠. East doesn't have enough to compete at the three level. South, with 11 high-card points and 2 length points for the six-card spade suit, jumps to 4♠.

OPENING LEAD

West leads the ♥A against 4♠, the top of touching honors against a suit contract.

BRIDGE QUIZ:

How can the defenders get two potential diamond tricks?

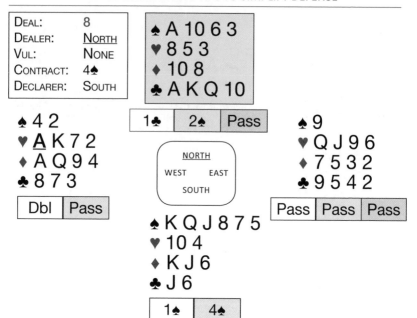

DEAL:	8
DEALER:	NORTH
VUL:	NONE
CONTRACT:	4♠
DECLARER:	SOUTH

♠ A 10 6 3
♥ 8 5 3
♦ 10 8
♣ A K Q 10

♠ 4 2
♥ A K 7 2
♦ A Q 9 4
♣ 8 7 3

| 1♣ | 2♠ | Pass |

NORTH
WEST   EAST
SOUTH

♠ 9
♥ Q J 9 6
♦ 7 5 3 2
♣ 9 5 4 2

| Dbl | Pass |

| Pass | Pass | Pass |

♠ K Q J 8 7 5
♥ 10 4
♦ K J 6
♣ J 6

| 1♠ | 4♠ |

SUGGESTED DEFENSE

East wants to encourage West to continue hearts and plays the ♥Q. The play of an honor when partner is winning the trick shows the next lower-ranking honor and denies the next higher-ranking honor.

West wants to put East on lead to play a diamond and, knowing East holds the ♥J, plays the ♥2 at trick two. East gains the lead with the ♥J and, looking at the dummy, plays the ♦7 rather than a club. This traps declarer's ♦K and the defense gets both the ♦A and ♦Q.

SUGGESTED PLAY

If the defenders don't take their diamond winners quickly, declarer can draw trumps and then discard two diamonds on dummy's extra club winners.

CONCLUSION

The play of the ♥Q on the ♥A shows the ♥J. East, the weakest hand at the table, plays an active role in defeating the contract by showing West where East's entry lies so the partnership can take a defensive diamond finesse.

DEAL #9

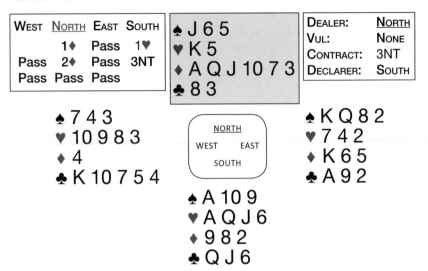

West	North	East	South
	1♦	Pass	1♥
Pass	2♦	Pass	3NT
Pass	Pass	Pass	

♠ J 6 5
♥ K 5
♦ A Q J 10 7 3
♣ 8 3

DEALER:	NORTH
VUL:	NONE
CONTRACT:	3NT
DECLARER:	SOUTH

♠ 7 4 3
♥ 10 9 8 3
♦ 4
♣ K 10 7 5 4

NORTH
WEST   EAST
SOUTH

♠ K Q 8 2
♥ 7 4 2
♦ K 6 5
♣ A 9 2

♠ A 10 9
♥ A Q J 6
♦ 9 8 2
♣ Q J 6

SUGGESTED BIDDING

North has enough to open 1♦ with 11 high-card points plus 2 length points for the six-card diamond suit. South, with 14 high-card points, responds 1♥, planning to get to game on the rebid. North rebids the six-card suit, and now South settles for game in 3NT.

OPENING LEAD

West is on lead against 3NT.

BRIDGE QUIZ:

What is the challenge if West leads the fourth best club against 3NT, hoping to get enough tricks through length to defeat the contract?

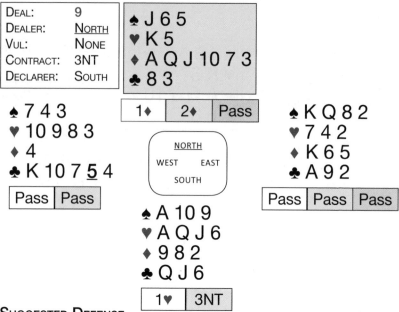

DEAL:	9
DEALER:	NORTH
VUL:	NONE
CONTRACT:	3NT
DECLARER:	SOUTH

♠ J 6 5
♥ K 5
♦ A Q J 10 7 3
♣ 8 3

| 1♦ | 2♦ | Pass |

♠ 7 4 3
♥ 10 9 8 3
♦ 4
♣ K 10 7 <u>5</u> 4

Pass | Pass

NORTH
WEST   EAST
SOUTH

♠ K Q 8 2
♥ 7 4 2
♦ K 6 5
♣ A 9 2

Pass | Pass | Pass

♠ A 10 9
♥ A Q J 6
♦ 9 8 2
♣ Q J 6

| 1♥ | 3NT |

SUGGESTED DEFENSE

West leads the ♣5, fourth best from the long suit. East wins the ♣A and returns the ♣9, higher of the two remaining clubs. South plays the ♣Q. West knows South also has the ♣J. East would return the ♣Q or ♣J if holding the ♣Q-9 or ♣J-9.

To establish and take the club winners, West needs an entry to the winners once they are established. Since West has no entry other than the ♣K, West has to hold up on the second club trick, playing the ♣4. West has to hope East has another club and will gain the lead before declarer has nine tricks. When East gains the lead with the ♦K, East still has the ♣2 to return. The defense gets the ♦K, ♣A, ♣K, and two more club tricks through length.

SUGGESTED PLAY

Declarer should play the ♣Q at trick two to tempt West into winning the ♣K.

CONCLUSION

To get tricks through length, the defenders often need to keep an entry within the long suit in case partner can gain the lead, and has a link card to reach the winners.

DEAL #10

WEST	NORTH	EAST	SOUTH
			1♥
Pass	3♥	Pass	4NT
Pass	5♥	Pass	6♥
Pass	Pass	Pass	

♠ A J 6
♥ J 10 8 4
♦ A J 10 9
♣ 7 5

DEALER:	SOUTH
VUL:	E-W
CONTRACT:	6♥
DECLARER:	SOUTH

♠ 8 7 5 3 2
♥ 6 3
♦ 2
♣ 10 6 4 3 2

NORTH
WEST   EAST
SOUTH

♠ K Q 9 4
♥ A 7
♦ 7 6 5 4 3
♣ J 9

♠ 10
♥ K Q 9 5 2
♦ K Q 8
♣ A K Q 8

SUGGESTED BIDDING

South opens 1♥ with 19 high-card points plus 1 length point for the five-card heart suit. North makes a limit raise to 3♥ with four-card heart support and 11 high-card points plus 1 dummy point for the doubleton club, showing about 10-12 points.

South can see slam is likely as long as the partnership is not missing two aces. South uses Blackwood and, when North shows two aces, South bids 6♥, knowing the partnership is missing only one ace.

OPENING LEAD

West is on lead against 6♥.

BRIDGE QUIZ:

Why does the fate of the deal rest with West, who doesn't have a single point?

What decision should West make for the opening lead?

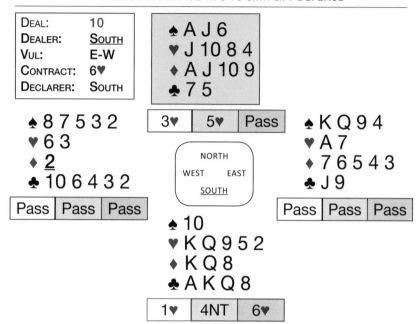

DEAL:	10
DEALER:	SOUTH
VUL:	E-W
CONTRACT:	6♥
DECLARER:	SOUTH

♠ A J 6
♥ J 10 8 4
♦ A J 10 9
♣ 7 5

3♥	5♥	Pass

♠ 8 7 5 3 2
♥ 6 3
♦ 2
♣ 10 6 4 3 2

NORTH
WEST   EAST
SOUTH

♠ K Q 9 4
♥ A 7
♦ 7 6 5 4 3
♣ J 9

Pass	Pass	Pass

Pass	Pass	Pass

♠ 10
♥ K Q 9 5 2
♦ K Q 8
♣ A K Q 8

1♥	4NT	6♥

SUGGESTED DEFENSE

West leads the singleton ♦2, expecting to take one defensive trick by ruffing a diamond. Since the opponents used Blackwood and stopped in a small slam, there's a reasonable expectation East will hold an ace.

West's lead of the singleton ♦2 gives the defense a chance. East should win the first heart trick with the ♥A and return a diamond. There's little point switching to the ♠K. The best hope is West has a singleton and can ruff the second diamond.

SUGGESTED PLAY

After the ♦2 lead, declarer wins the ♦A from the dummy. Now when declarer draws trumps, East has to immediately take the ♥A and return a diamond while West still has a trump left.

CONCLUSION

The lead of a singleton can often be effective against a trump contract, especially when the auction suggests there is a reasonable chance partner can gain the lead before declarer can draw all the trumps.

DEAL #11

West	North	East	South
			1NT
Pass	3NT	Pass	Pass
Pass			

♠ 8 4
♥ 10 5 3
♦ A K 7 5
♣ K J 9 6

DEALER:	SOUTH
VUL:	E-W
CONTRACT:	3NT
DECLARER:	SOUTH

♠ K Q J 9 6
♥ A 6
♦ J 10 4
♣ 7 4 2

```
        NORTH
  WEST        EAST
        SOUTH
```

♠ 5 3 2
♥ Q 9 8 2
♦ 8 6 3 2
♣ 5 3

♠ A 10 7
♥ K J 7 4
♦ Q 9
♣ A Q 10 8

SUGGESTED BIDDING

South opens 1NT with a balanced hand and 16 high-card points. West shouldn't come into the auction with a balanced hand, especially vulnerable. North, with 11 high-card points, has enough to raise to 3NT.

OPENING LEAD

West is on lead against 3NT and leads the ♠K, top of the solid sequence.

BRIDGE QUIZ:

Why is East key to defeating the contract when West's hand is so much stronger?

DEAL:	11
DEALER:	SOUTH
VUL:	E-W
CONTRACT:	3NT
DECLARER:	SOUTH

♠ 8 4
♥ 10 5 3
♦ A K 7 5
♣ K J 9 6

3NT

NORTH

WEST   EAST

SOUTH

♠ K Q J 9 6
♥ A 6
♦ J 10 4
♣ 7 4 2

Pass	Pass

♠ 5 3 2
♥ Q 9 8 2
♦ 8 6 3 2
♣ 5 3

Pass

♠ A 10 7
♥ K J 7 4
♦ Q 9
♣ A Q 10 8

1NT	Pass

SUGGESTED DEFENSE

West leads the ♠K, top of touching cards from a solid sequence. That's a good lead, however, this deal is all about the diamonds. Declarer has eight tricks and needs only one more. It will come from the diamond suit if East discards a diamond when declarer takes the club winners. East must keep the same diamond length as dummy to prevent dummy's fourth diamond, the ♦7, from becoming a winner.

SUGGESTED PLAY

Declarer has a spade, three diamonds, and four club tricks. Declarer's basic plan is to hold up the ♠A, until the third round and then hope to get a ninth trick by leading toward the ♥K. However, declarer should first take the club winners, keeping track of diamonds in case dummy's fourth diamond becomes a winner. Then there is no need to get a heart trick.

CONCLUSION

The defenders try to keep the same length in suits declarer might try to establish. On this deal, East is the only defender who can guard the diamond suit.

DEAL #12

West	North	East	South
			1NT
Pass	3NT	Pass	Pass
Pass			

♠ Q 9 5
♥ A K
♦ 10 7 5 3 2
♣ K 10 6

DEALER:	SOUTH
VUL:	NONE
CONTRACT:	3NT
DECLARER:	SOUTH

♠ 10 7 4
♥ Q J 8 6 5
♦ A 4
♣ Q 8 7

NORTH
WEST   EAST
SOUTH

♠ 8 6 3 2
♥ 7 4
♦ K 6
♣ 9 5 4 3 2

♠ A K J
♥ 10 9 3 2
♦ Q J 9 8
♣ A J

SUGGESTED BIDDING

South opens 1NT with a balanced hand and 16 high-card points. North, with 12 high-card points plus 1 length point for the five-card diamond suit, has enough to raise to 3NT.

OPENING LEAD

West leads the ♥6, fourth highest from longest and strongest, against 3NT.

BRIDGE QUIZ:

Why does second hand low not apply to East when declarer plays a low diamond from the dummy?

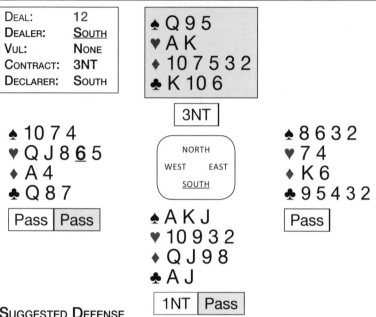

DEAL:	12
DEALER:	SOUTH
VUL:	NONE
CONTRACT:	3NT
DECLARER:	SOUTH

♠ Q 9 5
♥ A K
♦ 10 7 5 3 2
♣ K 10 6

3NT

NORTH

WEST   EAST

SOUTH

♠ 10 7 4
♥ Q J 8 **6** 5
♦ A 4
♣ Q 8 7

Pass | Pass

♠ 8 6 3 2
♥ 7 4
♦ K 6
♣ 9 5 4 3 2

Pass

♠ A K J
♥ 10 9 3 2
♦ Q J 9 8
♣ A J

1NT | Pass

SUGGESTED DEFENSE

With the high hearts in dummy, West knows East's attitude toward hearts. Declarer wins the first heart trick and East gives a count signal. Declarer next leads a diamond from dummy. East should forget the 'second hand low' maxim and play the ♦K, hoping to gain the lead and return a heart to help establish West's suit. If South holds the ♦A, East is unlikely to get a trick with the ♦K by playing low.

When West gains the lead with the ♦A, West can take the established heart winners to defeat the contract.

SUGGESTED PLAY

With only seven sure winners, declarer needs to promote two diamond winners to make the contract. Declarer has to hope West started with only four hearts or West doesn't have an entry after the hearts are established.

CONCLUSION

The defenders need to keep an entry with the long suit they are trying to establish, just as declarer does. East's only chance to win a trick and preserve partner's entries comes at trick two. East must make an exception to automatically playing second hand low.

DEAL #13

WEST	NORTH	EAST	SOUTH
			1♥
Pass	1♠	Dbl	3♥
Pass	4♥	Pass	Pass
Pass			

♠ K Q J 2
♥ 10 3
♦ K 6 5 2
♣ 10 9 8

DEALER:	SOUTH
VUL:	E-W
CONTRACT:	4♥
DECLARER:	SOUTH

♠ 9 8 6 3
♥ 6 2
♦ J 10 9 7
♣ Q 6 4

NORTH
WEST   EAST
SOUTH

♠ A 10 5
♥ J 8
♦ A Q 8 4
♣ K 7 3 2

♠ 7 4
♥ A K Q 9 7 5 4
♦ 3
♣ A J 5

SUGGESTED BIDDING

South opens 1♥ with 14 high-card points plus 3 length points for the seven-card heart suit. North, with 9 high-card points but only a doubleton heart, shows the spade suit. East has an opening bid with support for both unbid suits and makes a takeout double.

South makes a jump rebid of 3♥, showing a medium-strength hand of about 17-18 points and a good six-card or longer suit. North has enough to take the partnership to 4♥.

OPENING LEAD

West leads the ♦J, top of the solid sequence, against 4♥.

BRIDGE QUIZ:

How can West help East on defense when declarer plays a spade toward the dummy to promote the spade winners?

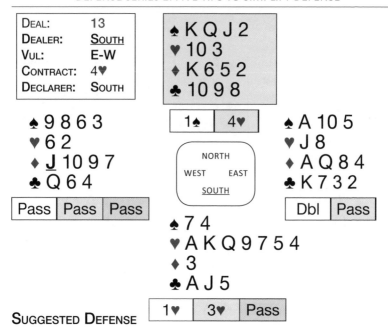

DEAL:	13
DEALER:	SOUTH
VUL:	E-W
CONTRACT:	4♥
DECLARER:	SOUTH

♠ K Q J 2
♥ 10 3
♦ K 6 5 2
♣ 10 9 8

♠ 9 8 6 3
♥ 6 2
♦ J 10 9 7
♣ Q 6 4

1♠	4♥

NORTH
WEST   EAST
SOUTH

♠ A 10 5
♥ J 8
♦ A Q 8 4
♣ K 7 3 2

Pass	Pass	Pass

Dbl	Pass

♠ 7 4
♥ A K Q 9 7 5 4
♦ 3
♣ A J 5

1♥	3♥	Pass

SUGGESTED DEFENSE

Knowing East holds the ♦A from West's lead of the ♦J, declarer plays low from dummy at trick one. East makes an encouraging signal with the ♦8. West continues with the ♦10, and declarer again plays low from dummy, East plays the ♦4, and declarer ruffs.

Declarer draws trumps in two rounds and then leads a spade. West should give a count signal by playing the ♠9, the start of a high-low signal showing an even number of spades. That tells East declarer likely started with only two spades, so East should hold up winning the ♠A for one round. The defenders eventually get a spade, a diamond, and two club tricks.

SUGGESTED PLAY

Declarer has a spade, a diamond, and two club losers. If East wins the first spade, declarer can discard a club loser on dummy's extra spade winner. If East doesn't win the second round of spades, declarer won't lose a spade.

CONCLUSION

Despite the weak hand, West has an important role to play by letting partner know how the spade suit is divided.

DEAL #14

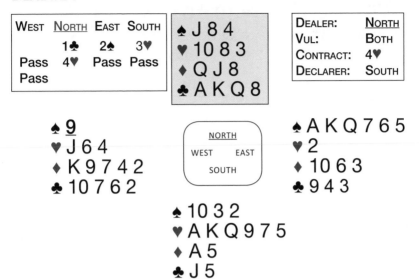

WEST	NORTH	EAST	SOUTH
	1♣	2♠	3♥
Pass	4♥	Pass	Pass
Pass			

♠ J 8 4
♥ 10 8 3
♦ Q J 8
♣ A K Q 8

DEALER:	NORTH
VUL:	BOTH
CONTRACT:	4♥
DECLARER:	SOUTH

♠ 9
♥ J 6 4
♦ K 9 7 4 2
♣ 10 7 6 2

NORTH
WEST   EAST
SOUTH

♠ A K Q 7 6 5
♥ 2
♦ 10 6 3
♣ 9 4 3

♠ 10 3 2
♥ A K Q 9 7 5
♦ A 5
♣ J 5

SUGGESTED BIDDING

North opens 1♣ with 13 high-card points and no five-card major. With a good six-card spade suit but only 9 high-card points plus 2 length points for the six-card suit, East makes a preemptive 2♠ jump overcall.

South has 14 high-card points plus 2 length points for the six-card heart suit. That's more than enough to bid 3♥, forcing. North, with three-card heart support, raises to 4♥.

OPENING LEAD

West leads the ♠9, the singleton in partner's suit.

BRIDGE QUIZ:

When East wins the first three spade tricks, how does West plan to defeat the contract?

How does West communicate the plan to East?

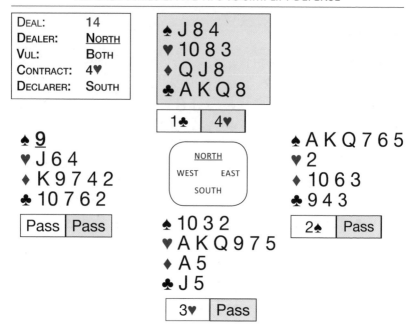

DEAL:	14
DEALER:	NORTH
VUL:	BOTH
CONTRACT:	4♥
DECLARER:	SOUTH

♠ J 8 4
♥ 10 8 3
♦ Q J 8
♣ A K Q 8

| 1♣ | 4♥ |

♠ 9
♥ J 6 4
♦ K 9 7 4 2
♣ 10 7 6 2

NORTH
WEST   EAST
SOUTH

♠ A K Q 7 6 5
♥ 2
♦ 10 6 3
♣ 9 4 3

| Pass | Pass |

| 2♠ | Pass |

♠ 10 3 2
♥ A K Q 9 7 5
♦ A 5
♣ J 5

| 3♥ | Pass |

SUGGESTED DEFENSE

East wins the first three spade tricks and West, looking at dummy, has to decide where the fourth defensive trick is coming from. Although West has the ♦K, that's not a sure trick. Holding the ♥J, however, a heart winner can be promoted if East leads a fourth round of spades.

To get East to lead another spade, West should discard the ♣2 and also the ♦2, both discouraging signals. This sends the message to East the only chance for a fourth trick is in hearts, the trump suit. If East leads a fourth round of spades, declarer can't prevent West from getting a trick with the ♥J.

SUGGESTED PLAY

If East doesn't lead a fourth round of spades, declarer can win whatever East returns, draw trumps, and discard the diamond loser on an extra club winner in dummy.

CONCLUSION

West must use Defenders' Plan to decide where the fourth trick is coming from and then send the appropriate signals to communicate the plan to East.

DEAL #15 – FAMOUS DEAL

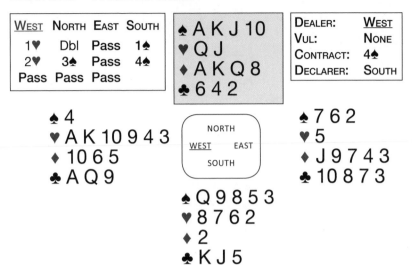

WEST	NORTH	EAST	SOUTH
1♥	Dbl	Pass	1♠
2♥	3♠	Pass	4♠
Pass	Pass	Pass	

♠ A K J 10
♥ Q J
♦ A K Q 8
♣ 6 4 2

DEALER:	WEST
VUL:	NONE
CONTRACT:	4♠
DECLARER:	SOUTH

♠ 4
♥ A K 10 9 4 3
♦ 10 6 5
♣ A Q 9

NORTH
WEST   EAST
SOUTH

♠ 7 6 2
♥ 5
♦ J 9 7 4 3
♣ 10 8 7 3

♠ Q 9 8 5 3
♥ 8 7 6 2
♦ 2
♣ K J 5

SUGGESTED BIDDING

West opens with 1♥ with 13 high-card points plus 2 length points for the six-card heart suit. North has 20 high-card points and support for the unbid suits. North makes a takeout double. East passes, and South advances to 1♠.

West has enough to compete to 2♥. North shows a very strong hand with a jump raise to 3♠ – South might have nothing. South, with 6 high-card points and a length point for the fifth spade, has enough to go on to 4♠.

OPENING LEAD

West is on lead against 4♠.

BRIDGE QUIZ:

What would West lead?

What should happen at trick two?

What should happen at trick three?

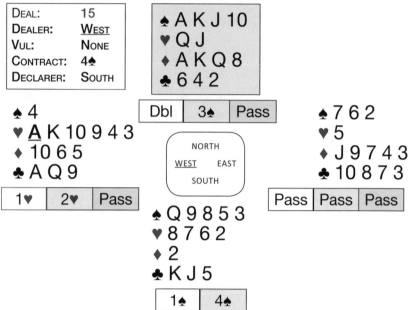

DEAL:	15
DEALER:	WEST
VUL:	NONE
CONTRACT:	4♠
DECLARER:	SOUTH

♠ A K J 10
♥ Q J
♦ A K Q 8
♣ 6 4 2

♠ 4
♥ A K 10 9 4 3
♦ 10 6 5
♣ A Q 9

| Dbl | 3♠ | Pass |

NORTH

WEST   EAST

SOUTH

♠ 7 6 2
♥ 5
♦ J 9 7 4 3
♣ 10 8 7 3

| 1♥ | 2♥ | Pass |

| Pass | Pass | Pass |

♠ Q 9 8 5 3
♥ 8 7 6 2
♦ 2
♣ K J 5

| 1♠ | 4♠ |

SUGGESTED DEFENSE

West leads the ♥A, top of the touching honors. After winning the first trick, West continues with the ♥K. East can see the defense isn't getting any more heart tricks so the only hope is for the defense to get two club tricks. Unless West holds the ♣A-K, clubs need to be led by East. East has to ruff the second heart and lead a club so the defenders can take a defensive club finesse.

SUGGESTED PLAY

Declarer plans to ruff two heart losers in dummy and discard two clubs on dummy's diamonds, losing only two hearts and a club.

CONCLUSION

East has the weakest hand at the table but uses the only opportunity to gain the lead for a defensive club finesse.

When this famous deal was played, it was common to lead the king from ace-king. West, Al Sobel, led the ♥K followed by the ♥A. Although players are warned not to trump partner's ace, Al Sobel's wife, the great Helen Sobel, ruffed the ♥A and led a club. At the end of the deal, Al said, "Thanks for ruffing my ace!"

DEAL #16 – FAMOUS DEAL

WEST	NORTH	EAST	SOUTH
Pass	1♦	Pass	1♠
Pass	2♦	Pass	3NT
Pass	Pass	Pass	

♠ 6 4
♥ A 7 5
♦ K 10 9 8 5 3
♣ A 3

DEALER:	WEST
VUL:	NONE
CONTRACT:	3NT
DECLARER:	SOUTH

♠ J 10 5
♥ J 9
♦ A 6 4
♣ K 9 8 6 2

NORTH
WEST   EAST
SOUTH

♠ 9 8 3 2
♥ Q 10 8 6 3
♦ Q 2
♣ Q 7

♠ A K Q 7
♥ K 4 2
♦ J 7
♣ J 10 5 4

SUGGESTED BIDDING

After West passes, North opens 1♦ with 11 high-card points plus 2 length points for the six-card diamond suit. South responds 1♠. North rebids the six-card diamond suit and South, with 14 high-card points and stoppers in the other suits, jumps to 3NT.

OPENING LEAD

West is on lead against 3NT.

BRIDGE QUIZ:

What would West lead?

What will East do after winning the first trick?

How can the defenders prevent declarer from establishing the diamond suit?

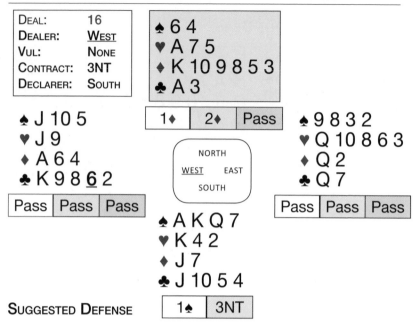

DEAL:	16
DEALER:	WEST
VUL:	NONE
CONTRACT:	3NT
DECLARER:	SOUTH

♠ 6 4
♥ A 7 5
♦ K 10 9 8 5 3
♣ A 3

1♦	2♦	Pass

NORTH

WEST   EAST

SOUTH

West hand:
♠ J 10 5
♥ J 9
♦ A 6 4
♣ K 9 8 6 2

Pass	Pass	Pass

East hand:
♠ 9 8 3 2
♥ Q 10 8 6 3
♦ Q 2
♣ Q 7

Pass	Pass	Pass

South hand:
♠ A K Q 7
♥ K 4 2
♦ J 7
♣ J 10 5 4

SUGGESTED DEFENSE

1♠	3NT

West leads the ♣6, fourth best. Declarer plays low from dummy, East wins the ♣Q and returns a club, driving out the ♣A. Declarer comes to the South hand with a spade and leads the ♦J, playing low from dummy when West plays low. To defeat 3NT, East has to play a low diamond! Declarer repeats the diamond finesse by playing a diamond to dummy's ♦10. This time East wins the ♦Q. Declarer can no longer establish the diamonds.

SUGGESTED PLAY

With three spades, two hearts, and a club winner, declarer plans to establish extra diamond tricks, starting with a finesse against the ♦Q. If this loses, declarer can drive out the ♦A to establish enough tricks with the ♥A as an entry.

CONCLUSION

When East wins the second diamond trick with the ♦Q, the ♦A is still held by West. Declarer can use the ♥A to get to dummy and play another diamond to drive out the ♦A, but now there is no entry to the dummy to get to the diamond winners.

Eric Murray, Canadian Silver Medalist, was the defender who smoothly ducked holding the doubleton ♦Q.

Glossary

Attitude Signal—A defensive carding signal to let partner know whether you want a particular suit led. A high card is an encouraging signal; a low card is a discouraging signal. (Page 5)

Auction—The process of determining the contract through a series of bids. (Page 1)

Balanced Hand—A hand with no voids, no singletons, and no more than one doubleton. (Page 31)

Blocked—A suit in which the winners cannot be taken immediately because of entry problems. (Page 6)

Broken Sequence—A sequence of cards in a suit where the third card from the top is missing, but not the next lower-ranking card(s). For example: ♥K-Q-10-9, ♦J-10-8. (Page 33)

Count Signal—A defensive signal showing an odd or even number of cards in a suit. In standard methods, a high-low signal shows an even number of cards; a low-high signal shows an odd number. (Page 5)

Defenders' Plan—Similar to Declarer's Plan, for the defenders. There are three suggested stages, the ABCs: Assess the Situation, Browse Defenders' Checklist, and Consider the Order. (Page 11)

Entry—A way to get from one hand to the opposite hand. (Page 1)

Finesse—A method of building extra tricks by trapping an opponent's high card(s). (Page 12)

Fourth Highest—A lead of the fourth card down from the top in a suit. (Page 4)

Hold Up—Letting the opponents win a trick that you could win. (Page 17)

Honor—An ace, king, queen, jack or ten. (Page 1)

Interior Sequence—A holding in a suit that contains a sequence and a higher-ranking card that is not part of the sequence. For example: ♥A-J-10-9, ♦Q-10-9-8. (Page 4)

Keep an Entry—When developing tricks through promotion or length, declarer needs to keep an entry to the hand that will have the established winners. (Page 16)

Length—The number of cards held in a suit. Also, the development of tricks through exhausting the cards the opponents hold in a suit. (Page 1)

Opening Lead—The card led to the first trick. The player to declarer's left leads first. (Page 1)

Promotion—Developing one or more cards into winners by driving out any higher-ranking cards held by the opponents. (Page 12)

Raise—Supporting partner's suit by bidding the suit at a higher level. (Page 23)

Ruff(ing)—Play a trump to a trick when holding no cards in the suit led. Same as trumping. (Page 4)

Rule of Eleven—When partner leads the fourth highest card in a suit, subtracting the number of the card led from eleven gives the number of higher cards in the remaining three hands. Since you can see how many higher cards are in dummy and in your hand, you know how many higher cards declarer holds. (Page 4)

Second Hand Low—A popular guideline when playing second to a trick after a low card has been led is to also play a low card, keeping high cards to capture the opponents' high cards. (Page 15)

Short Side—The partnership hand with fewer cards in a specific suit. (Page 12)

Signals—Conventional plays made by the defenders to give each other information. (Page 5)

Solid Sequence—Three or more consecutive cards in a suit headed by an honor. For example: ♥K-Q-J-10, ♦Q-J-10-5. (Page 4)

Strength—The point count value of a hand. (Page 1)

Suit Preference Signal—A defensive signal made when following suit that indicates preference for another suit. (Page 5)

Support—Cards held in a suit that partner has bid. (Page 2)

Sure Trick—A trick that can be taken without giving up the lead to the opponents. (Page 6)

Third Hand High—A popular guideline when playing third to a trick is to play only as high as necessary to win the trick for the partnership. (Page 15)

Top of Nothing—The lead of the top card from a holding of three or more cards with no honor in the suit. (Page 2)

Unblock—Play or discard a high card that is preventing you from taking winners in a suit. (Page 1)

Notes